Based on a true story

RHYTHMS FOR RUBY

written by
Karen Callaway Williams

ISBN: 1439273308
ISBN-13: 9781439273302

When tragedy happens around us, most often we wonder what we can do to help. We want to do something to make a wrong thing right and put things back to normal or at least, lighten a load or help remove a burden. Sometimes the problem is so big that we believe that we can't fix it ourselves. But sometimes we try anyway using the gifts and talents that God gave us. And someone comes along and sees us trying and helps us with the gifts and talents that God gave them. And someone else comes along and sees us trying and begins to help in their God given way. And then others come and see us and decide to help as God leads them. And after a while the huge problem is dwarfed by the multitude of people who decided that they could have a hand in diminishing a huge problem using the gifts that God gave them...until it is no longer a problem.

Thank you for being a part of the multitude of people who decided to have a hand in diminishing a huge problem.

Karen Callaway Williams

Show and Tell

Gabriella was so excited by her first dance recital. She went back to school the next day to tell her class about the experience. Her classmates were excited to see her pictures, her colorful, sparkly costumes, and her tap dance shoes that made a clickety clack sound. Even the boys were excited to see real tap shoes because they knew about tap dance. They had seen Savion Glover on Sesame Street. Everyone in her class was excited..... Except for Ruby.

It wasn't that Ruby wasn't happy for her friend, Gabriella. It was just that earlier that year she had been in a terrible car accident and was now in a wheel chair because she had lost one of her legs. She could still walk with her crutches, but the wheelchair made it easier for her to get around the classroom. She was happy for Gabriella, but she knew that she would never be able to have the same experience as Gabriella. When Ruby went home she prayed, "Dear Lord, I know that I can trust you. I know you have something special planned for me and my life. I know that you are always with me to give me a little more courage and strength. And I know that you love me no matter what. I love you too, Amen!"

Gabriella went home and told her mother about her wonderful day at school. She told her how excited the other children had been about the pictures, her costumes and the sounds that her tap shoes had made on the classroom floor. She told her about how brave they thought she was for being able to stand on stage and dance in front of people. Gabriella beamed. "That's wonderful dear," her mother smiled. "I am so glad that you had a fantastic day. I am proud of you because you did a great job at your recital yesterday. What did Ruby say about your presentation?"

Gabriella stopped and looked at her. "Ruby liked it", she said. "She said that she was proud of me and that she thought that I was really brave to dance in front of an audience." "But mom," Gabriella said, "With all that Ruby is going through right now, Ruby is much braver than I am!"

The Final Dance Class

The next day after school, Gabriella went to her final dance class of the year. The children sat in a circle with their teacher, Miss Karen, to talk about the experience of their first dance recital. Each child told of how the recital had affected them.

William said that he loved it and that he wanted to do it again tomorrow.

McKenzie said that she had been so nervous that she hadn't slept at all the night before.

Hanna said that afterwards her grandma had given her a beautiful bouquet of flowers that she kept in her bedroom, in a vase, on a dresser.

Adam said that he was glad that he had practiced a lot because he felt prepared when the day arrived.

When Gabriella's turn came to tell of her impressions of the day, she decided to tell of the day after the recital of her "show and tell" time at school.

She talked about the reaction of her classmates, but she shared that she was saddened because she realized that one of her friends in the classroom, Ruby, would not be able to tap dance because she only had one leg because of an accident.

"Oh", Miss Karen said. "Did I ever tell you about the famous one legged tap dancer Clayton "Peg Leg" Bates?" " Who?" the class asked all at once. "Clayton "Peg Leg" Bates," Miss Karen said with a smile.

"Clayton "Peg Leg" Bates was an African-American tap dancer from Fountain Inn, South Carolina. He was born in 1907. In 1918 when the men in his town and family went off to fight in World War I, Clayton begged his mother to let him work in the cotton mills to help make money to support his family. After praying for three days, his mother said yes to his request. One night, while he was at work, one of the lights went out towards the back of the factory and he was sent to change it. On his way he stepped into the machinery by accident and had to lose part of his leg, but because he was young and had a mind to continue to be active, his uncle made him a "peg leg" so that he could learn to run and play like the other children. He also learned to dance, tap dance and went on to be in movies, on television, and on stages across the world."

"Wow, Miss Karen," Gabriella said. "That gives me an idea."

When Gabriella got home, she told her mother about her tap class and all that Miss Karen had said about Clayton "Peg Leg" Bates. "Peg Leg Bates," Gabriella's mother said. "I remember him. We used to watch him on television. He was amazing!"

Her mother told her about another dance show on television in which one of the dancers had had only one leg, but had a special leg made to match so that she could dance with two legs. The dancer had moved so gracefully that her mother had not been able to tell which leg had been her special leg.

"I want Ruby to have a special leg too," Gabriella said. "I want her to be able to dance and run and play just like she did before."

"That would be great," her mother said with a smile.

"Where do you get a special leg mom?" Gabriella asked.

"I'm not sure exactly," her mother said, "but we could find out tomorrow."

That night, Gabriella prayed. "Dear Lord, please help us to get a special leg for Ruby, Amen."

Help Me Please

The next day at school, Gabriella saw Ruby. She told her about what Miss Karen had said about Clayton "Peg Leg" Bates being a tap dancer. She also told her about the woman that her mother had seen on television.

"I have a special leg," Ruby said.

"You do," Gabriella said? "Why don't you wear it?"

"I don't like to wear it. It looks like a stump. It's ugly and it hurts."

"Oh," Gabriella said.

"It doesn't even match my skin." Ruby said. Before the accident, I had nice legs and I liked to show them off by wearing skirts and dresses. Now, I don't want to show my legs at all."

"Where did you get your special leg?" Gabriella asked.

"At the hospital," Ruby said.

"Couldn't you get a leg that matched and one that wasn't ugly?" Gabriella asked.

"It would have to be specially made and they are really expensive." Ruby said. "My family is still trying to pay for all of the hospital bills."

7

"Oh" Gabriella said.

That night Gabriella prayed, "Dear Lord, I want Ruby to have a special leg. She should have a cute one that matches her other leg and one that doesn't hurt. She said that they were expensive and so she doesn't have one, but I want her to have one. Help me please! Amen." For the next few hours, Gabriella thought and thought until she fell asleep.

Get Right To It

The next morning Gabriella woke up with an idea.

"Mom, I have a great idea!" Gabriella announced at breakfast. "I want to have a fund raiser to raise money for a new leg for Ruby!"

"That's a great idea," her mother said. "What do you want to do? What kind do you want to have? Do you want to have a car wash, a bake sale, or a penny drive?" her mother asked.

"No," Gabriella said. "I want to have a tap dance show."

"A tap dance show," her mother asked?

"Yes, a tap dance show," Gabriella beamed, "and I want to call it Rhythms for Ruby."

"That's a great name for a show," Gabriella's mother said. When would you like to have your fund raiser, Gabriella?"

Gabriella looked at the calendar. "How about one month from Saturday?"

"Four weeks!" her mother said with alarm. "That's not a lot of time!"

"Well, I guess I just have to get right too it," Gabriella exclaimed!

9

When Gabriella got to school, she told her teacher, Mrs. Stevens, about the idea that she had to have a fund raiser for Ruby.

"That's a fantastic idea, Gabriella. When do you want to have it?" Mrs. Stevens asked.

"Four weeks from Saturday," Gabriella said.

"That doesn't give you a lot of time," her teacher said. "I'll tell you what we can do. I will take you to the school office at lunch time to see if that date is available to use the auditorium for the show," she said.

"That sounds great!" Gabriella said jumping up and down and clapping her hands.

Gabriella could hardly concentrate while waiting for the lunch bell to ring. After the rest of the class went to the lunchroom, she and Mrs. Stevens walked to the office.

"Good afternoon Mrs. Stevens. Good afternoon Gabriella," the school secretary said. "How may I help you today?" she smiled.

"I want to have a tap dance show to raise money to purchase a special leg for my friend Ruby. I would like to know what I'd have to do to use the auditorium and if it's available on the date that I've chosen."

"Well that sounds like a wonderful idea," the secretary said. "Now let me look at my calendar." After a few moments, she said with a nod, "that date is available so far. Now you must go to see Principal Marsh and also speak with the drama teacher because she's in charge of all of the activities that happen on the stage."

Gabriella's heart sank and began to pound. "I have to see the Principal, Mr. Marsh!" she asked with alarm.

"Oh yes," the secretary said. "He has to know about all of the activities that take place at the school. He's not in right now, but he'll be in tomorrow."

"Thank you," Gabriella said nervously.

Gabriella walked back to the cafeteria with Mrs. Stevens. Her heart was still beating fast. She was afraid to see the principal. He was really tall. He spoke loudly when he made the announcements over the intercom system, and he had seemed so serious in assembly programs!

As she and Mrs. Stevens walked into the cafeteria, the drama teacher was walking out.

"Oh Mrs. Sims," Gabriella said. "Excuse me please."

Mrs. Sims stopped and looked at her.

"I would like to have a fund raising concert, four weeks from Saturday in the auditorium. It's for my friend Ruby, the girl in my class who lost her leg in the accident. The office secretary said that I had to speak with you."

"What did Principal Marsh say?" Mrs. Sims asked.

"He's out of the office until tomorrow," Gabriella said. "I have to see him tomorrow."

"Well, stop by my classroom before you leave today to pick up a form for your mother to fill out. Bring it back tomorrow. I will check my calendar to be sure that the stage is not being used. I will let you know tomorrow."

"OK, thank you," Gabriella said.

After lunch, the day flew by. Gabriella was excited that the date was available on the secretary's calendar, but she was nervous about talking to Principal Marsh. She picked up the form from the drama teacher before she left to go home.

While waiting on the school bus to go home, Gabriella watched as Ruby struggled to get from her wheel chair into her mother's car.

On the way home, she prayed, "Dear Lord, help me. I'm afraid to talk to Principal Marsh, but Ruby needs a leg. Help me not to lean toward my fear side but to lean towards my courage side. Amen."

Mr. Marsh's Office

The next day, Gabriella got up and put on her favorite pink outfit. She took her time arranging her hair and she brushed her teeth twice. When she got to school, Mrs. Stevens told her that they would go to see Mr. Marsh at lunch time. When the bell rang, she took a deep breath and stood up. She was still very nervous. She wasn't sure of what she would say to Mr. Marsh and she was afraid of what he might say. As she and Mrs. Stevens walked the rest of the class to the cafeteria, Gabriella watched as Ruby pushed herself in her wheelchair. She thought of how they used to play before the accident and even though things would not be the same, a special leg would definitely make things better for her.

Gabriella and Mrs. Stevens knocked on the door of Mr. Marsh's office.

"Come in please," his voice boomed! "Hello Gabriella, Mrs. Stevens," he said with a bright smile as he stood up. "I've been expecting you. Please sit down."

Gabriella had never before seen him smile and thought that he had a kind face when he did. She sat down.

"So I hear that you want to have a fund raiser for Ruby," he said. "Please tell me all about it."

Gabriella began to speak. "I would like to have a fund raiser for Ruby, so that she might have a special leg, a cute one that matches her skin and doesn't hurt. She has trouble getting in and out of the car and she's always in a wheel-chair. She can't run and play like she used to and even though she has crutches; it would be great if she could walk without them."

"I want to have a tap dance show because I just had my first recital and it was great! I want to call the show "Rhythms for Ruby!""

"Rhythms for Ruby," Mr. Marsh said. "That's quite a catchy name, Rhythms for Ruby." he said again.

"I spoke with Mrs. Sims this morning," Mrs. Stevens said. "It's alright with her if it's alright with you. I would be available to help too."

"Well that's a fine idea. I only wish that it weren't strictly a tap dance show," he said. "I would love to play my banjo in the show."

"You can, Mr. Marsh," Gabriella said. "I was talking to my mom last night and she said that I should include more people in the show using the gifts and talents that God gave them. "Your rhythm is tap dance," my mom said, but other people show their rhythm in different ways. If you would let other people bring their different rhythms together, it would be an amazing and wonderful show, Rhythms for Ruby."

"Wow, "Mr. Marsh said sitting back. That is an outstandingly generous idea. I will help get the word out to my friends," he said. "When do you want to have it?"

"Four weeks from tomorrow," Gabriella said.

"Although that doesn't give us much time," he said, you are welcome to have it. I think that it is a great idea, and please Gabriella, let me know what I can do to help."

He stood up and held out his hand with a smile. She stood up and shook it.

"Ruby has a great friend in you," he said.

"Thank you," she smiled and went back to the lunch room with Mrs. Stevens with a huge smile on her face. "Thank you Lord," she said quietly.

In the cafeteria Gabriella found Ruby and told her everything.

"You went to Principal Marsh's office?" Ruby said with alarm.

"He's going to play the banjo," Gabriella chuckled.

"Well, everyone has their own rhythm," Ruby said.

"He's really very nice and he has a very nice smile..." Gabriella went on.

It Takes Money

When Gabriella got home, she told her mother everything.

"Well, you know Gabriella, sometimes to have a fund raiser you have to raise money to support all of the parts of the fund raiser. If you want to have a show in a theater, you often have to rent the theater, although, you already have been promised the school auditorium. Actually, that was the reason for the special form from Mrs. Sims."

"If you want to advertise by handing out colorful flyers, you have to buy the colored paper, glitter, glue and markers. If you want to put an announcement in the newspaper, sometimes you have to pay for it."

"Hmm, I hadn't thought about that mom," Gabriella said.

"You could have a fund raiser to raise funds for the fund raiser. You could bake cookies and sell them in front of Mr. Peterson's store," her mother said. "Of course, you would have to ask Mr. Peterson first."

"I like Mr. Peterson," Gabriella said.

"You could use half of the money that you raise to buy paper for posters, flyers and supplies and the other half could go to Ruby. As you sell the cookies, you can tell about the concert and invite people to come."

"I like that idea, mom," Gabriella said.

"Tomorrow is Saturday. We could go to see Mr. Peterson after breakfast and after you clean your room," her mother said.

"I'll clean my room tonight!" Gabriella said.

Mr. Peterson was happy with the idea of the bake sale. It was for a good cause and he was glad to be able to help. I will see you next Saturday morning," he said.

On Monday morning Gabriella told Mrs. Stevens about the cookie sale.

"You should allow the class to bake and sell their favorite cookies," she said.

Mrs. Stevens told the class about the cookie sale and they were very excited.

"I want to make sugar cookies," Michelle said.

"My favorites are peanut butter," said Zachary.

"I like chocolate chip," said Daniel.

"I made gingerbread cookies with my grand-mother," Lulu said. "I want to make those."

"When are we having it?" Jonathan asked.

"We don't have much time so it will be on Saturday," Mrs. Stevens said. "I will make permission slips for your parents to sign and tell the type of cookies that they want to bake. Each bag of three cookies will be sold for two dollars. One dollar will go to Ruby and one dollar will go for fund raising supplies."

On Saturday morning, the cookie sale was a complete success. Lots of people were out shopping and were interested to hear about Ruby and the show. By one o'clock, all of the cookies were sold.

On Monday morning, Mrs. Stevens told the class how proud she was of them and that they had done an excellent job at baking and selling cookies.

The Sign Up Sheet

At lunchtime Ruby said, "Gabriella, did you see the sign up sheet on the bulletin board by the cafeteria door?"

"What sign up sheet?" Gabriella asked.

"The sign up sheet that Mrs. Sims, the drama teacher, posted, so that people could perform in the fund raiser. Come and look!"

Gabriella walked to the cafeteria door as she pushed Ruby along in her wheelchair. The hall monitor stopped them at the door.

"Where do you think you're going?" he asked.

"We would like to see the sign up sheet for the fund raiser, just outside this door," Gabriella said.

"Oh, alright," the hall monitor said. "Lots of people have been stopping by to sign up all through lunch."

She rolled Ruby out the door. Sure enough, there were seven solos, duets and groups signed up on the paper.

One student signed up to play the piano. Another group signed up to do a karate demonstration. Two little girls signed up to do a ballet duet and another student signed up to do magic tricks with an assistant. Of course, the first name written at the top of the list was Mr. Marsh and beside his name was written BANJO.

"Wow," Gabriella said. "This is really happening! Oh Ruby, this is so exciting! There really is going to be a show. I am going to call my tap dance teacher, Miss Karen, and tell her that I want our entire class to be in this show too, so we can sign up tomorrow."

When Gabriella went home, she told her mother about the sign up sheet and asked if she could call Miss Karen.

"Let me look for her phone number," she said.

Gabriella dialed the number and waited.

"Hello," Miss Karen answered.

"Hello Miss Karen. This is Gabriella from your tap dance class."

Hello Gabriella," Miss Karen said brightly. How are you? What's on your mind today?"

"We are having a fund raiser at my school for my friend Ruby, The girl in my class that I told you about when you spoke about Clayton "Peg Leg" Bates. It's a show and I want our entire tap dance class to do the dance that we did in the recital."

"That's a great idea," Miss Karen said. The best way to use your gifts and talents is to serve someone else. Let me get in touch with their parents and I will call you back. When is the fund raiser?"

"Three weeks from Saturday at seven o'clock," Gabriella said.

"That doesn't give us a lot of time to practice, but it will be fine. I think that it is great that you want to include the other children too. I will start calling their parents now and schedule a rehearsal."

"Miss Karen," Gabriella said, "the show is called Rhythms for Ruby!"

"What a fun name for a show"! Miss Karen said. "I will call you back!"

The next day at lunch time Gabriella went to the bulletin board and signed up for the fund raiser to dance with her tap dance class. All of the children, but one, were available to participate in the show. She noticed now that eleven groups of people had signed up and her group was number twelve.

School-wide Event

After lunch, Mrs. Stevens announced that the class would take part in one more fund raiser before the big event. This fund raiser would be a penny drive. She asked the class to bring in a coffee can with a lid. They would decorate the can in art class the next day. Then, they would each take their tin can and flyers announcing the show door to door in their neighborhoods collecting pennies and telling their neighbors about Ruby and the fund raiser. As other teachers in the school heard about the penny drive, they decided to have their classes get involved as well. It soon became a school wide event. The students brought coffee cans to school and decorated them in art class. For the next week and a half, students brought cans to school full of pennies from moms and dads, sisters and brothers, aunts and uncles, grandparents, friends and neighbors, and the information continued to spread about Ruby and the fund raiser.

After three days, Mr. Marsh set up a special savings account at the local bank called "The Rhythms for Ruby Account" because they could no longer keep the pennies at the school. The word spread about the fund raiser so much that it caught the attention of a news reporter at the local paper.

What's Your Rhythm?

News reporter Gerald Joe Nance called the school to inquire about the fund raiser.

"Oh," the school secretary said. "You should speak with Mrs. Stevens and the two students in her class Gabriella and Ruby."

"When would be the best time to speak with them?" he asked.

"Probably at lunchtime," the secretary said. "Actually, let me contact Mrs. Stevens and I will call you back," she said.

"Lunch time would be perfect," Mrs. Stevens said. During their quiet class time, I will contact their mothers to make them aware of the interview.

By lunchtime, all was arranged and at the agreed upon time Mr. Nance came to the classroom.

"Mrs. Stevens, hello, my name is Gerald Joe Nance and I am a reporter with the local paper."

"Hello, Mr. Nance," Mrs. Stevens said. "This is Gabriella and this is Ruby."

"It is my pleasure to meet both of you, and because of the two of you, there's quite a stir in the community. Please tell me how all of this started."

Ruby told Mr. Nance about the longstanding friendship that she had with Gabriella. She told him about the accident and how it had affected her life and her family's lives.

Gabriella told of her desire to help her friend walk again and to make her life a little easier. She told him how she wanted her friend to have a special leg that matched her skin and that didn't hurt. And she told him how the fund raiser, Rhythms for Ruby, could help make that happen.

Mrs. Stevens added details of the cookie sale and the penny drive and that all donations were welcomed.

"How did you come up with the name of the show?" Mr. Nance asked.

"Everyone has a different rhythm," Gabriella began. "For some people it's dancing or singing, for some it is drawing or painting. Others find their rhythm in karate or sports. And still others have their rhythm in sharing their money or in writing news stories," she smiled looking at him. "Whatever a person's rhythm, we've invited them and the entire community to come and bring their rhythms together to support and help Ruby. Rhythms for Ruby!!!!"

"Wow, Mr. Nance said. That is a clever idea and this is going to be a fantastic news story. This story is worth reporting. I'll get right on it. When is the show? I can't wait to come."

"Next Saturday at 7 pm," Gabriella said.

"I look forward to it," Mr. Nance said. "I will put this story out right away. Before I leave, let me take a picture of the three of you, he said. Smile!"

On Sunday morning, Gabriella's mother woke her with excitement in her voice. "Gabriella wake up," her mother said as she shook her. "You are on the front page of the news paper!" she squealed.

"I am? She asked, still sleepy, rubbing her eyes.

"Yes," her mother said. "Your Rhythms for Ruby story is front page news."

"Let me see!" Gabriella exclaimed. "Oh mom, I have to call Ruby!" she said excitedly.

Gabriella called Ruby. "Did you see the paper?" Gabriella asked.

"Yes, we are reading it right now," she said. "My father just went out to buy twenty more copies for relatives."

"It tells about everything," Gabriella said. Mr. Nance really has a rhythm for writing a great news story."

"He sure does," Ruby said.

"Well, I'll see you later," Gabriella said. "I have to get ready for church."

"Me too", Ruby said. "I'll talk to you later. Bye!"

On Monday morning the entire school was talking about the news story. There was a feeling of excitement in the air. Throughout the week the students and teachers were busily working on the last minute details.

On Friday, there was a rehearsal in the auditorium and all of the performers were eager to see each other!

Say Yes and Follow Through

On Saturday morning, Gabriella received a call from Ruby.

"Hello," Gabriella said.

"Hello Gabriella, this is Ruby," she said.

"Hi, what's up?" she asked.

"I just wanted to thank you for everything. So much is happening so quickly and it is all very exciting. As I said my prayers last night, I thought of you and I knew that all of this would not have happened if it weren't for you. I just wanted to say thank you. I am really lucky to have a friend like you."

"That's OK," Gabriella said. "I'm lucky to have you as my friend too. I've learned a lot."

"I knew that God loved me and that he had something very special for me. But you had to say yes to the idea of a fund raiser and follow through," Ruby said. I really, really appreciate you! I could actually be walking again soon!

"You're welcome. I'm glad that I did," Gabriella said.

"Well I know that you are getting ready for tonight, so I'll see you later."

"OK," Gabriella said. "See you tonight." "Goodbye." "Thank you Lord," Gabriella said quietly.

Rhythms for Ruby

The audience was full of parents and neighbors and relatives and friends. It seemed that the entire town had come out. Mrs. Stevens introduced each act and told jokes along the way. Mr. Marsh was really great at playing the banjo and the crowd went wild with applause for him. Gabriella's tap dance class did an even better job than they had done at the recital. Ruby and her family sat in the front row amazed. It was a magnificent evening!

Near the end of the show, Ruby and her parents were called to the stage to be presented with a check. All of the money collected from the cookie sale, the penny drive, the ticket sales and donations was more than enough to pay for all of Ruby's medical bills.

As Ruby was about to leave the stage, Mrs. Stevens stopped her. "Please wait here," she said. "Gabriella, please come to the stage," Mrs. Stevens said on the microphone. When Gabriella came to the stage, Mrs. Stevens, Miss Karen, and another woman were waiting for her.

"Gabriella," the woman said. "My name is Melody Bates-Holden. I'm a friend of Miss Karen and "Peg Leg" Bates was my father. She told me about what you were doing for your friend and I was impressed. On behalf of my family and your community, we would like to present you with The Clayton "Peg Leg" Bates Humanitarian Award. And Ruby, because of the generosity of your community, YOU WILL HAVE a cute leg that matches your skin and that doesn't hurt!"

Gabriella and Ruby hugged each other and bounced with glee!

The audience stood up and erupted with applause!!!

Mrs. Stevens and Miss Karen wiped tears from their eyes.

Within a year, Ruby walked into Miss Karen's tap dance class on her new leg ready for her first tap dance lesson.......

The End

Written by Karen Callaway Williams
Text Copy written 2008

Special Thanks and Recognition to:
GOD, for all things!!!
Miss Ruby Blount
Melodye Bates Holden
Clayton "Peg Leg" Bates
Rev. Rose Dean
Mrs. Renee Williams